MAJOR DISASTERS
in U.S. History

Steven Otfinoski

Reading Advantage Authors
Laura Robb
James F. Baumann
Carol J. Fuhler
Joan Kindig

Project Manager
Ellen Sternhell

Editor
Jeri Cipriano

Design and Production
Preface, Inc.

Photography and Illustration
Front cover, p. 40 © AP Photo/Jack Smith; pp. 1, 9, 23, 32b © Bettmann/Corbis; pp. 12, 44 map art by Sue Carlson; p. 13 © Corbis; pp. 16, 26 © The Granger Collection; p. 29 © Underwood & Underwood/Corbis; pp. 32t, 42 © AP Photo; p. 37 © Paul A. Souders/Corbis; p. 46 © Alan Weiner/Liaison/Getty Images.

Copyright © 2005 by Great Source Education Group, a division of Houghton Mifflin Company. All rights reserved.

No part of this work may be reproduced or transmitted in any form or by any means, electronic or mechanical, including photocopying and recording, or by any information storage or retrieval system without the prior written permission of Great Source Education Group, unless such copying is expressly permitted by federal copyright law. Address inquiries to Permissions, Great Source Education Group, 181 Ballardvale Street, Wilmington, MA 01887.

Great Source® is a registered trademark of Houghton Mifflin Company.

International Standard Book Number: 0-669-51416-0

3 4 5 6 7 8 9 10 – RRDC – 09 08 07 06 05

CONTENTS

Introduction — 4

Chapter 1 Chicago on Fire — 6

Chapter 2 The Plague of the Locusts — 14

Chapter 3 The Blizzard of '88 — 20

Chapter 4 The *Hindenburg* Tragedy — 27

Chapter 5 Mount St. Helens Blows Its Top — 35

Chapter 6 A Hurricane Named Hugo — 43

Introduction

Disasters have struck the world since its earliest days. Earthquakes, fires, storms, floods—we have endured them all. These disasters have destroyed homes and buildings. These disasters have killed animals and people. Disasters of all kinds have created confusion and chaos. But we have survived!

Until recent years, people had little defense against natural disasters. Today, modern technology and science help scientists predict when some storms will strike. So people sometimes can be evacuated from an area and find safety. But technology can't always help. Storms and other events can be destructive and deadly. Scientists have yet to be able to predict exactly when an earthquake will happen.

It isn't just Mother Nature's power that we have to deal with. We also have to face disasters caused mostly by human error. People sometimes make mistakes—bad ones. And the cost of those mistakes can be life itself.

I have included both natural disasters and human-caused disasters in this book. Hurricanes, blizzards, volcano eruptions, and insect invasions are natural disasters. The Great Chicago Fire and the Hindenburg disaster were mostly caused by human error.

As terrible as they are, disasters often bring out the best in people. We step up to show how caring we are toward other human beings. We show courage that sometimes surprises even us. We rescue, rebuild, and celebrate life. This is the amazing power of the human spirit to survive.

CHAPTER 1

Chicago on Fire

Fire was a frequent problem in America before the twentieth century. Most buildings and homes were made of wood, so they easily caught fire. Firefighting equipment was crude by today's standards. It couldn't do the job of putting out major blazes. And firefighters had little training and few skills. So large fires usually ended up as disasters.

Of the thousands of fires in American towns and cities, one remains the most famous. It was the fire that engulfed the city of Chicago in October 1871.

The summer and fall of that year had been unusually hot and dry with little rainfall. Chicago had as many as seven fires a day. The night of October 7, a lumber mill caught fire and a four-block area burned. It took every one of Chicago's twenty-nine fire companies about sixteen hours to put out the blaze. It was the worst fire of the year. But it would hold that title for less than twelve hours.

A Fire Starts in a Barn

The next day was a warm and windy Sunday. The O'Leary family on DeKoven Street on the southwest side of the city turned in early. Tomorrow was another workday, and they needed their sleep.

Around 8:45 PM, a fire broke out in the O'Learys' barn behind the house. No one knows for certain how the fire started. One of the cows may have kicked over a kerosene lamp. A family boarder, Dennis Sullivan, who was known to sometimes drink too much, may have been responsible.

Whether he set it or not, Sullivan was the first one to see the fire. He was almost its first victim. His wooden leg became caught in a crack in the barn floor and came off. He held on to the neck of a fleeing calf to get out of the burning barn.

The fire might have been put out before it grew much larger. But a string of human errors helped it spread swiftly. Soon after Sullivan spread word of the fire, a neighbor ran to a corner drugstore to report a fire alarm. The storeowner refused to give him the key to the alarm box. He said that the fire had already been reported. But that wasn't so.

Soon after, a fire watchman spotted the growing blaze, but he miscalculated where it was. He sent firefighters a mile away from the O'Learys' barn. He later realized his mistake. His assistant refused to send another alarm. The assistant thought that it would only confuse the firefighters.

The Fire Spreads

It wasn't until about 9:30 PM that the first fire company arrived on the scene. The wind and a strong updraft created by the fire swept up burning materials and embers into the air. These spread the fire to other city blocks. The fire was quickly growing out of control.

Exhausted by the previous night's fire, firefighters struggled to contain this new one. Authorities hoped that the blaze would be stopped as it headed east by the south branch of the Chicago River. But by the time the fire reached there, it was so massive and intense that it leaped over the river. Then it moved steadily toward the heart of downtown Chicago.

An hour earlier, people were watching the fire with curiosity. Now, many of them were packing up whatever belongings they could carry and running away from the fire.

One young girl, Claire Innes, was fleeing with her family through the crowded streets. She later wrote, "I felt as a leaf . . . in a great rushing river."

This illustration from a newspaper of the time captures the fear and panic people experienced during the Great Chicago Fire.

One of the fire's many heroes was politician James Hildreth. Hildreth was armed with 2,500 pounds of dynamite and began exploding houses. He wanted to create a gap of open space that would stop the fire dead in its tracks. The strategy stopped the fire from moving southward. But the explosions couldn't create enough open space to halt the fire's movement to the east.

The City Burns

Firefighters continued to fight the blaze as best they could. Then, at 3 AM on Monday morning, the fire reached the waterworks building. As it burned, the four pumping engines shut down. Chicago had no water. There was no chance to stop the fire now.

A fifth of the city's population was fleeing for their lives. Some headed west, where the fire was not traveling. Others moved south to the shores of Lake Michigan. Still others rushed farther north to the safety of Lincoln Park, which was by the lake.

As people fled, buildings burned. One after another, city landmarks fell to the flames. The main post office building and Crosby's Opera House disappeared. So did the Grand Pacific Hotel, still under construction, and the supposedly "fireproof" *Chicago Tribune* building.

By noon on Monday, the fire had reached the edge of Lincoln Park. The intense heat and smoke drove many people into the lake. They stood up to their necks in the cold water and watched their city burn.

The fire burned all Monday. It must have seemed to many that it would not end until every building in Chicago had been consumed. Then, at about 11 PM, rain began to fall. It only drizzled, but by 3 AM, a steady downpour was falling. The rain eventually put out most of the fire, although small fires continued to burn for days.

The fire was over, but it had taken a heavy toll. Smoke and fire had killed at least three hundred people. Some 17,500 buildings were destroyed. Ironically, among the homes left standing was the O'Leary house, a few yards away from where the fire had started. The O'Learys and other poor people on the South Side were unfairly blamed for the fire.

Total property damages came to $200 million. Nearly one hundred thousand people were left homeless. Of that number, about a third found temporary shelters or left the city to start over somewhere else. Among the people who left were the O'Learys. They were driven away by those who blamed them for the fire.

This map shows the large area of the city destroyed by the Great Chicago Fire.

After the Fire

The first one on the scene to help was the famous Civil War general Phil Sheridan. His troops gave out tents and other needed supplies to the homeless. Within a few days, trainloads of food, clothing, and cash were coming in from all over the country and Europe. The Chicago Relief and Aid Society built five thousand homes within a month of the fire and found jobs for more than twenty thousand workers.

The rebuilding of the city was soon underway. It provided steady work for thousands of carpenters, bricklayers, and other laborers. The new Chicago that arose from the ashes of the old was bigger and bolder. It was built of brick and stone, not wood, and was made to last. Chicago became the great city it is known as today.

Lake Michigan and the city skyline today

CHAPTER 2

The Plague of the Locusts

Grasshoppers are fascinating insects. They can "sing" by rubbing their legs together. They can jump the distance of twenty times their body length. This is how they earned their name. But grasshoppers also can be very destructive. Short-antennae grasshoppers, called locusts, are especially disastrous. When they come together in a large swarm, they can eat through a field of crops in no time.

In the summer of 1874, a locust plague descended on the Great Plains of the United States. It so happened that there was a long drought that summer. Farmers were able to grow some crops, but not many. Then along came the locusts.

The first people who saw the locusts must have thought a dust storm was on the way. Billions of the insects formed dark clouds in the sky. They came from the west, carried over the Rocky Mountains by strong winds. For this reason, they were called the Rocky Mountain locusts.

The Locusts Move In

The locusts were so thick in the air that at times they covered the sun. Day turned into night. When the cloud of locusts descended, billions of "hoppers," as they were called, covered the ground. The insects first attacked fields of corn. They ate every cob and kernel. Next, they devoured every kind of grain, vegetable, and fruit. When these were gone, they dug into the ground and ate root vegetables like potatoes and bulbs of flowers. Then they chewed their way through weeds and the leaves and bark of trees.

When the locusts had eaten all the plant life, they attacked leather harnesses, the wood in farm tool handles, and cotton curtains. These nasty insects would even eat the shirt on a person's back!

One farmer described the locusts "as thick as snowflakes in a storm." He added that ". . . they drifted along with the breeze, and fluttered down at your feet occasionally, or lit on your nose."

To keep the locusts from crawling up their legs, farmers tied strings around their pants cuffs. They clamped their hats down on their heads to keep the insects out of their hair.

The locusts even interfered with transportation. They were attracted to the warm railroad tracks in the morning. When the train rolled by, its wheels crushed the locusts. Their slimy bodies made it impossible for the train wheels to get enough traction to move. Passengers could be stuck for hours, while the crew threw sand on the tracks to get enough traction to move again.

Farmers fought locusts to save their crops and livelihood.

Fighting Back

Farmers fought back in every way they could. Some covered their crops with blankets or burned smudge pots, containers where oil is burned to protect against insects and frost. They hoped the thick smoke would drive away the locusts. Others let loose their horses, cows, and hogs from the barn to crush the locusts underfoot. This plan backfired. The animals ate so many of the locusts that they got sick. When the animals were killed, their flesh had the unpleasant odor of the locusts. Their meat was not fit to eat.

Some people decided to eat the locusts themselves as a strange kind of revenge. First they pulled off the legs and wings of dead locusts. Then they roasted them over a fire or boiled them in stews and soups. Some people fried them with salt, pepper, and butter. The grasshoppers made a tasty snack that was rich in protein. Some Native Americans ate grasshoppers as a regular part of their diet. Many farmers, however, could not bring themselves to eat the creatures that were threatening their livelihood.

All these ways to stop the locusts largely failed. More successful were specially made machines.

The simplest machine was a long, shallow pan filled with coal tar and oil. The pan was mounted on wheels and rolled or pushed along the ground. The locusts hopped into the pan to get out of its path. They drowned in the tar and oil.

More effective was a machine that literally sucked up the locusts like a vacuum cleaner. It then hurled them against a wire screen. Their dead bodies fell into a bag. Another machine caught the locusts and crushed them between two large rollers.

For four summers, the dark clouds of locusts came down on Kansas, Missouri, and other Great Plains states. They destroyed more than two hundred million dollars' worth of crops. Some farmers gave up and headed back East, but most stuck it out and stayed. They received food, clothing, and money from the government and from people living in other states.

Then, in 1877, the locusts began to dwindle in number. By about 1900, the Rocky Mountain locust variety disappeared as mysteriously as it had appeared. Today, this variety is thought to be extinct.

But locust plagues continue today in other parts of the world. Locusts have regularly attacked farmland in Africa and Asia. Today, pesticides and other chemicals kill some locusts but not all of them. The plague goes on.

CHAPTER 3

The Blizzard of '88

Saturday, March 10, 1888, was the warmest day of the warmest winter in New York City in seventeen years. New Yorkers were eagerly looking forward to an early spring. The forecast for Sunday was "cloudy, followed by light rain and clearing."

The rain came, but it became increasingly heavy as the day wore on. Temperatures began to fall rapidly, and the wind became fierce and cold. Two massive weather systems were on a collision course. Arctic air was moving down from Canada. And a warm, moist air mass was coming up from the Gulf of Mexico. The two met around the Chesapeake Bay area, creating a monster of a storm.

The first effects of the storm were felt at sea. Ships and boats were tossed and overturned by driving winds and swelling waters. By late Sunday, the storm was heading straight for New York City. Sometime after midnight, the rain in the city turned to snow.

Snow, Snow, and More Snow

Millions of New Yorkers awoke Monday morning, surprised to see all the snow. "The air looked as though some people were throwing buckets full of flour from all the rooftops," said one man. Few people, however, realized just how big this storm would be. If they did, many more might have stayed at home.

As the morning wore on, the snowfall grew heavier. It was helped along by huge gusts of wind. Wind reached speeds of eighty-five miles per hour. Visibility became so poor that an elevated train on the Third Avenue Line crashed into a stalled train. One person was killed and fourteen were injured in the accident.

Soon after, the elevated trains stopped running. An estimated fifteen thousand people were stranded high above the city streets in train cars. Enterprising men set up ladders under the cars. For a quarter, the men assisted each passenger down to safety. Other people showed up with ladders. Soon the price for a climb down a ladder soared to two dollars.

By late afternoon, many workers faced the grim prospect of a long walk home in the blizzard. Some businesses, like Macy's department store, set up cots for workers to stay the night.

Not everyone took advantage of this offer. Two women factory workers in Bridgeport, Connecticut, turned down an offer to stay the night at work. They left together and soon found themselves lost in the swirling snow. The two women were found a day later in a snowdrift only a few yards outside the factory gate. They were frozen to death, locked in each other's arms.

Many others fell victim to the blizzard, too. Former New York Senator Roscoe Conkling, a strong and healthy man, started walking from his downtown Wall Street office to his home uptown. A friend walking with him wisely gave up the struggle. The friend stopped for the night at a hotel along the way. Conkling continued on alone.

Conkling became stuck up to his shoulders in a snowdrift for twenty minutes. He finally made it home, only to die five weeks later from the effects of his ordeal. He was the storm's most famous victim.

Others managed to survive through their resourcefulness. A man in New Haven, Connecticut, gave up trying to walk home. He dug a cave with his bare hands in the bottom of a snowdrift. He stayed there for the night and emerged safely the next day.

People brave the blizzard in downtown New York City. Note the tangle of icy telephone wires.

Many people collapsed in the snow from exhaustion and stress. A priest in New York City was returning from a sick call when he saw a hand sticking out of a snowdrift. It was one of his Sunday school students. The snow had overcome her, while she was looking for food for her family. The priest dug her out and carried her to safety.

Many trapped commuters sought warmth and refreshments in taverns. (The city had many taverns.) Theaters were shut down, with one exception. Showman P. T. Barnum's circus played its matinee and evening performances in Madison Square Garden. Only one hundred people were in the audience. "If only one customer had come, I would have given the complete show," Barnum boasted.

By Tuesday, the snow began to die down. However, it took days before the city was back to normal. A total of twenty-one inches of snow had fallen in New York. Totals to the north were far greater. Some thirty-seven inches fell in Springfield, Massachusetts. A total of fifty inches fell in Middletown, Connecticut, and fifty-five inches fell in Troy, New York.

After the Blizzard

Once the snow stopped falling, residents in several cities were faced with the problem of what to do with it. Some people in Newark, New Jersey, kept their sense of humor. They planted signs atop giant snowbanks. One sign read "500 Girls Wanted—To Eat Snow." Storeowners offered shoppers one thousand pounds of snow free with a one-dollar purchase. These offers went unanswered.

People in New York City shoveled for weeks. They shoveled snow into horse-drawn carts to be dumped into the East River. Nature helped out with warming temperatures that melted much of the snow.

If the storm had come earlier in the winter, the disaster would have been far worse. As it was, a total of four hundred people died in the storm, half of them in New York City. Another one hundred died at sea in more than two hundred shipwrecks. Property losses in New York alone were twenty million dollars. (And that was in 1888!)

But good things came out of the "white hurricane," as some called it. Authorities realized how vulnerable aboveground power lines and elevated trains were in a storm. The lines were eventually buried underground. In 1913, the first New York underground subway system opened.

As time passed, the Blizzard of '88 became a legend. Some of the stories told about it became exaggerated. However, they did not lessen the status of a storm that many scientists say comes only once every five hundred years.

No storm today could paralyze a city the way the Blizzard of 1888 did. Weather technology and mass communications would give people time to prepare. For those who lived through it, however, the Blizzard of '88 was indeed the storm of a lifetime.

This legendary blizzard paralyzed New York City like no other storm previously had.

CHAPTER 4

The *Hindenburg* Tragedy

On May 6, 1937, thirty-six people died in one of the most publicized disasters of modern times. With those deaths, a dream of flight died.

Before the Wright Brothers flew their first airplane in 1903, a German count had conquered the skies. He did so with a very different kind of flying machine. Count Zeppelin's airship had no wings. It floated across the sky like a giant balloon.

Unlike earlier hot-air balloons, however, Zeppelin's "airship" could carry many passengers. It could move across the sky with great speed. This airship consisted of several balloons contained inside a hollow, rigid structure. While it didn't have wings like a plane, the airship did have fins to help steer it. It also had engines to power its flight.

By 1914, the airships had carried more than 34,000 passengers on 1,600 flights around Germany.

During World War I, the airship was used in bombing raids. German airships dropped bombs over England, one of its enemies.

The New Airships

When Zeppelin died in 1917, Hugo Eckener, his leading pilot, took over his company. In 1928, Eckener built the *Graf Zeppelin,* named in the count's honor. It was 776 feet long and could travel at eighty miles per hour. Eckener flew the *Graf Zeppelin* across the Atlantic to the United States in 1929. The following year, he flew it around the world.

A few years later, Eckener built the largest zeppelin of all, the *Hindenburg*. It held twice the volume of gas as the *Graf Zeppelin* and had more than five thousand square feet of living space in its hull. There was room for seventy-two passengers.

The *Hindenburg* was more than an airship. It was a flying palace. It had a dining room that served the finest foods, a lounge, a promenade, or upper deck, with towering windows, and even a library. The *Hindenburg* and the other blimps like it were truly special. They were so beautiful and majestic that some people called them "cathedrals in the sky."

But Eckener's airships had one flaw. They were filled with hydrogen, a highly flammable gas. Helium, another gas that was not as flammable, could have been used instead. But hydrogen was cheaper. According to experts, it also gave the zeppelins more lift. Most importantly, the United States owned most of the world's helium. It would not sell the gas to Germany.

The *Hindenburg* was the biggest flying machine ever built.

Eckener's company knew the danger of hydrogen gas. Matches and anything that could produce a spark were forbidden on board. The walls of the hull were made of fireproof asbestos. So the zeppelins had a nearly spotless safety record. Not one paying passenger had been killed or injured in thousands of flights.

Tragedy in the Air

On May 3, 1937, the *Hindenburg* left Germany on its twenty-first crossing to North America. Strong headwinds slowed its flight. It arrived in New York City about ten hours behind schedule. As the airship crossed over the city, people looked up at it in awe. A baseball game in Brooklyn, New York, stopped so that players and spectators could watch the great airship pass overhead.

The *Hindenburg* headed south to its final mooring in Lakehurst, New Jersey. (The airships didn't land like modern airplanes. They were tied to a mooring—a tower of some kind.) The airship arrived there about 4 PM. Thunderstorms were in the area. The head captain steered the airship south to the New Jersey shoreline to wait out the storms.

The skies looked better around 7 PM, and the *Hindenburg* returned to make its landing. It came to a halt about 250 feet above the mooring. The crew dropped two ropes from the airship's nose to the ground crew below. Everything seemed normal and routine.

Then passengers looked out the windows and saw people on the ground pointing to the ship with fear on their faces. The tail of the airship was on fire. After a few moments, it crumbled apart and went crashing to the ground below.

By now the entire ship was burning. It descended slowly downward, a mass of flames. In about thirty-four seconds, the world's largest airship was in ruins.

Among the shocked spectators of this tragedy was Herb Morrison, a radio announcer. He was reporting the landing of the *Hindenburg* and stopped in mid-sentence as the flames appeared. "It's broken into fire!" Morrison cried. "It's flaming —flaming! This is terrible! This is one of the worst catastrophes in the world. Oh, the humanity and all the passengers!"

Radio broadcasts, newsreels, and photographs like these made the *Hindenburg* tragedy one of the best-documented disasters of its time.

As Morrison spoke, the passengers and crew were fighting for their lives. One passenger, a German acrobatic dancer, hung onto the outside of a window, waiting for the ship to get closer to the ground. When it did, he dropped off, landing safely.

Werner Franz, the fourteen-year-old cabin boy, was waiting for the ship to reach the ground when a water tank burst over his head. The water that drenched him helped save his life in the fire. He leaped to the ground and ran to safety. Another man hesitated to jump out of an open window and went back to find his wife in the burning ship. Both perished.

Perhaps the most astonishing tale of survival was that of an elderly couple, bags in hand, who appeared at the steps when the airship hit the ground. They walked calmly down the steps to the ground as if nothing was wrong. Although injured, they escaped with their lives.

In all, sixty-seven of the ninety-seven people aboard the *Hindenburg* survived the disaster. Five of them later died in the hospital. One member of the ground crew was also killed. It still was amazing that so many people were able to escape a fiery death.

The End of the Airships

Why did the *Hindenburg* explode into flames? If the hydrogen ignited, how did it do so? Hugo Eckener believed static electricity in the stormy air ignited hydrogen gas leaking from the back of the airship. Others believe that a time bomb sabotaged the airship. The fins of the *Hindenburg* had swastikas imprinted on them, emblems of Nazi Germany. Anti-Nazis may have seen the airship as a symbol of Nazi power and wanted to destroy it. However, no evidence of sabotage has ever been found.

Whatever the cause of the disaster, it spelled the end of the airships. The *Graf Zeppelin*, which had been making regular runs between Germany and Brazil, was immediately brought home and never carried passengers again. In 1940, during World War II, Germany demolished the *Graf Zeppelin*, along with the newer *Graf Zeppelin II*. Germany used the scrap from the ships for the war effort.

Today, the great German airships are but a distant memory. At the top of the Empire State Building in New York City, you can still see the tower built as a mooring for the great zeppelins. It was never used.

CHAPTER 5

Mount St. Helens Blows Its Top

Mike Moore was a nut for volcanoes. That's why, in early May 1980, he brought his wife and two young children on a camping trip to western Washington state. Just thirteen miles from their campsite was Mount St. Helens, a volcano in the Cascade Range. Mount St. Helens had shown signs of erupting for the past several months.

Moore wasn't too worried, though. Thirteen miles put them well outside the designated red danger zone. Besides that, there were three natural ridges between them and Mount St. Helens.

Then at 8:32 on a sunny Sunday morning, the trees in the forest that surrounded their campsite began to shake. All at once, the sky darkened, and a huge cloud of ash swept down the mountain toward the Moore family. Mike grabbed his camera. His wife, Lu, grabbed their two kids. "Once we saw the cloud coming our way, I never looked back," Lu Moore later said.

A Storm of Ash

Moore snapped off a dozen pictures. Then he followed his family into an empty hunter's shack. Ash, dust, and soil swirled around the shack like snowflakes in a blizzard. Small rocks pounded on the roof like hailstones. Lu covered their three-month-old with a blanket. The others held dampened socks to their faces so they could breathe.

The "storm" finally ended. But the sky was so filled with ash that it seemed day had turned into night. When it grew light enough to see, the Moores fled the shack. They began hiking to their car that was two and one-half miles away.

Giant trees felled by the blast soon blocked their path. It took the Moores more than five hours to cover just two miles. Suddenly, the trail disappeared, wiped out by the volcano's power. So they camped again for the night. The next day, they were spotted and picked up by a rescue helicopter.

The Moores could count themselves among the lucky ones that day. Some fifty-seven other people weren't so lucky. They didn't live to tell about their experience in the first major volcanic eruption in the lower forty-eight continental United States in nearly sixty years.

Thick, gray ash covered everything.

A Mountain of Fire

Mount St. Helens had long been considered one of the finest peaks in the Cascades. The Native Americans in the region respected and feared the mountain. They avoided going near it even though its green slopes were rich in game to hunt. They called it *Tah-one-lat-cluh*, "fire mountain" in English. They knew the beautiful mountain was actually a volcano that had been erupting regularly for at least 4,500 years. Layer after layer of hardened lava had given Mount St. Helens its symmetrical cone shape.

White settlers became aware of the mountain's fire for the first time in 1832. For more than two decades, it belched clouds of steam and lava occasionally. However, the mountain had been quiet since 1857. That all changed by 1975.

Geologists had been keeping an eye on the mountain for some time. In 1969, they predicted that it could erupt "before the end of this century." From 1975 to 1980, geologists at special stations in the region recorded forty-four small earthquakes. On Thursday, March 20, 1980, they recorded the strongest earthquake to date. One week later, a hole on the mountain's north side briefly erupted. It was time to take action.

The state governor declared an area up to about four miles from the summit a "red zone." Only government officials and scientists would be permitted in this zone. Several miles below this was declared a "blue zone." Homeowners who lived there and hundreds of lumberjacks who cut timber there could enter only during daylight hours.

Not every resident in the red zone was willing to leave. Eighty-three-year-old Harry Truman had lived on the shores of Spirit Lake for fifty-three years. "I am part of that mountain," he told authorities. "The mountain is part of me."

Time was running out. A bulge on the north side of the mountain was growing larger by the day. Scientists believed that hot liquid called *magma* from deep in the earth was collecting inside the mountain. By May 12, the bulge extended five hundred feet from the mountain's surface.

Like the Moores, David Johnston, a thirty-year-old volcanologist, was camping out at a station about five miles from the mountain's summit on that Sunday morning. At 8:32 AM, the geological headquarters in Vancouver, Washington, received an excited radio call from Johnston. "Vancouver, Vancouver, this is it." Then the voice broke off. David Johnston was never seen or heard from again. Like many victims, he probably suffocated when burning ash filled his lungs.

When the mountain erupted, the entire upper-north side of Mount St. Helens crumbled. It slid down into Spirit Lake. The mountainside hit the lake with such force that all the water was pushed up the other side of an adjoining ridge. When it flooded back into the lakebed, Spirit Lake was eighty feet lower than it had been before. Harry Truman's house was buried under forty feet of volcanic ash. Truman's body was never found.

The horizontal explosion on Mount St. Helens set off a second eruption. It blew off the top of the volcano. A column of ash and smoke rose twelve miles into the air. The fiery blast knocked down six million trees like they were toothpicks. The two eruptions killed five thousand deer, fifteen hundred elk, and two hundred black bears. Birds and small mammals were wiped out. Millions of salmon and trout were boiled alive in rivers and streams.

Mount St. Helens erupted with a force equal to ten million tons of dynamite on May 18, 1980.

Effects of the Eruption

Within a few hours, one of the most spectacular wilderness regions on Earth was transformed into a barren landscape. And the effects of the eruption were widespread. Windows rattled more than one hundred miles from the site. For twelve hours, ash fell like rain throughout the Northwestern United States and southern Canada. Cars crept through semi-darkness and people wore facemasks to breathe. Ash clogged machines and power transformers. The ash caused massive power failures in Washington, Idaho, and Montana.

While the destruction was terrible, the toll on human life could have been far worse. If the eruption had occurred twenty-four hours later on a Monday, hundreds of loggers would have been at work in the area. They would have been killed.

Ten days after the eruption, fresh deer tracks were seen on the mountain's south side. Within a month, a firewood blossom sprouted on a barren ridge near Spirit Lake. Trees and shrubs appeared from under melting snow banks.

Even more remarkable, some animals survived the volcano. Hibernating frogs and salamanders that were buried in the mud on the lake bottom were untouched.

Mount St. Helens Today

Today, Mount St. Helens is part of a one-hundred-thousand-acre national monument with a visitor's center. Thousands of tourists come through it yearly.

What scientists have learned from Mount St. Helens has helped them predict most of the next twenty-four eruptions worldwide.

All is quiet now in western Washington. Yet there are fifteen other volcanic mountains in the Cascade Range. Which one will blow its top next, and when? No one can say for certain.

This is Mount St. Helens as it looks today. Within three years, ninety percent of the plant life on Mount St. Helens had returned.

CHAPTER 6

A Hurricane Named Hugo

Hurricanes are among the most powerful storms on Earth. Born at sea, they are swirling dynamos of wind and water. These storms can reach wind speeds of more than 190 miles per hour. Few hurricanes in the twentieth century have done as much damage as Hurricane Hugo.

Like most hurricanes, Hugo came to life in the Atlantic Ocean. It originated somewhere off the coast of West Africa on September 10, 1989. Within a few days, Hugo became a full-fledged hurricane with sustained winds of seventy miles per hour.

The United States sent out a plane to measure the size and strength of Hugo. The crew expected to measure winds of up to 115 miles per hour. Instead, their plane was pounded by winds of 190 miles per hour. The crew had to dump fifty thousand pounds of fuel to lighten the plane enough to break free of the hurricane.

Meteorologists gained a new respect for Hugo. They named it a category five storm. This is the highest rating for a hurricane.

A Hurricane on the Move

On the night of September 17, Hugo was spinning west toward the Caribbean Islands. Just before midnight, it struck the islands of Guadeloupe and Montserrat. Twenty-one people were killed and twelve thousand left homeless. Hugo next slammed into St. Croix in the U.S. Virgin Islands.

By noon on September 19, Hugo struck the eastern tip of Puerto Rico. Twelve people were killed and more than thirty thousand left homeless. The island's mountains slowed down the hurricane. By the time it was at sea again, Hugo was weakening. The warm waters of the Gulf Stream brought Hugo back to life.

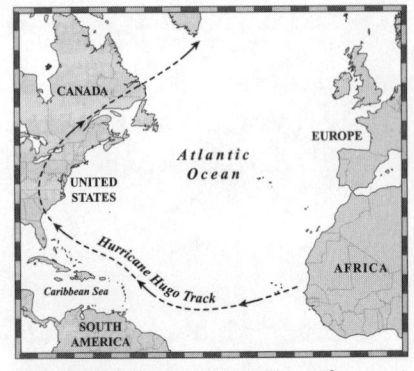

This map shows Hugo's path from Africa to the Caribbean to Canada.

Hugo was now heading for the South Carolina coast. Charleston, one of the South's most beautiful cities, lay directly in the storm's path. By noon on September 21, about 250,000 people were evacuated from coastal areas.

Hugo struck land near Charleston with a twenty-foot storm surge. It was the highest ever recorded on the East Coast. This large surge of water damaged more than half of Charleston's four thousand historic structures.

The brunt of the storm's fury, however, hit the rural area north of the city. The Francis Marion National Forest was flattened. Tens of thousands of trees were snapped off at fifteen to twenty feet above the ground. It was as if some giant buzz saw sliced through the area, leaving half-cut trees in its wake.

The barrier islands off the coast were also devastated. Beach homes were swept off their foundations. A road by the side of the ocean was stripped of its pavement. The Atlantic House, a popular island restaurant on the water, was completely swept away. All that remained were the pilings that supported it.

Hurricane Hugo's fury destroyed people's homes and lives.

Hugo did not spare those South Carolinian communities lying inland. Hundreds of residents of tiny McClellanville, three miles from the ocean, fled their homes. They found shelter on higher ground at the local high school.

Families huddled together and watched with horror as waters from the storm surge rose outside the school. The waters finally broke through the doors. Adults stood on tables and chairs to stay above the waters. They held their children in their arms.

The power went out at about 1 AM. In complete darkness, the terrified evacuees felt the water rising. Soon it was up to their necks. Many people swam out windows, rather than drown inside. Others stuck it out, lifting their children to the roof rafters. Incredibly, the waters receded. No lives were lost.

People in other inland communities were not so fortunate. Mobile homeowners eighty miles inland thought that they were safe. Winds of 120 miles per hour slammed across the countryside, wrecking 1,200 mobile homes and killing eight people.

A Costly Storm

As Hugo swept northward, it brought heavy rains to Virginia. Two million people in the state lost power. By late September 22, Hugo took its last breath. It died out in the cold air of southern Canada.

Hugo left thirty-five people dead and more than seven billion dollars in damages in the United States alone. Another forty people died in the Caribbean with three billion dollars in damages. It was the costliest hurricane in U.S. history at that time. It was the worst storm to strike Georgia and the Carolinas in a century.

Help was quick in coming. The federal government gave 1.1 billion dollars in aid. U.S. soldiers, marines, and National Guardsmen poured in to keep order and provide assistance. Thousands of volunteers called Hugo Busters came from as far away as California. They helped rebuild houses for 56,000 homeless people.

Hugo will stay in some record books for the destruction it caused and for its costs. But this hurricane will be remembered as much for people's courage and generosity in response to it. Once again, people showed what is best about the human spirit.